Ballet Class Valentines

Coloring & Craft Book

Written and Illustrated by Vanessa Salgado

©2023 Crafterina. All Rights Reserved.
Published by Crafterina
ISBN: 979-8-9868612-1-0
www.Crafterina.com

Create homemade

Valentines

Share your love of dance with a valentine!
This book was made to help you create the
sweetest homemade valentines to give your friends
and dance teachers. Inside you'll find coloring
pages, valentines, and craft activities designed
to spark imagination and inspire movement!

Enjoy crafting, moving, and sharing your
love of dance at ballet class!

Happy Valentine's Day!

For more dance and
valentine fun:

www.Crafterina.com

Valentine's Day at Ballet Class!

Best Friends

Ballet Besties

Happy Valentine's Day!

I heart you!

A rose for you!

Love to dance!

Be my Valentine!

www.Crafterina.com

Thanks for being
my friend!

Valentine's Day Dance Moves

Make a heart
with your hands

Make a heart
with your arms

Make a heart
with your feet

Best Friend Dances

Jump
for joy
together

Make a   heart   together

Let's create crafts and Valentines

Safety Note For Parents: All crafts require parent supervision to create. There are pieces to cut out that will require your help. Have fun creating together!

Tiara

Valentines

You're a great dancer!

Happy Valentine's Day!

Pop-Up Card

Paper Dolls

www.Crafterina.com

Create a Valentine

Directions: 1. Color Valentine 2. Cut out along dotted line 3. Personlize the back

Happy Valentine's Day!

Back of Valentine

To:

From:

Create a Valentine

Directions: 1. Color Valentine 2. Cut out along dotted line 3. Personlize the back

Happy Valentine's Day!

Back of Valentine

To:

From:

Create a Valentine

Directions: 1. Color Valentine 2. Cut out along dotted line 3. Personlize the back

Happy Valentine's Day!

Back of Valentine

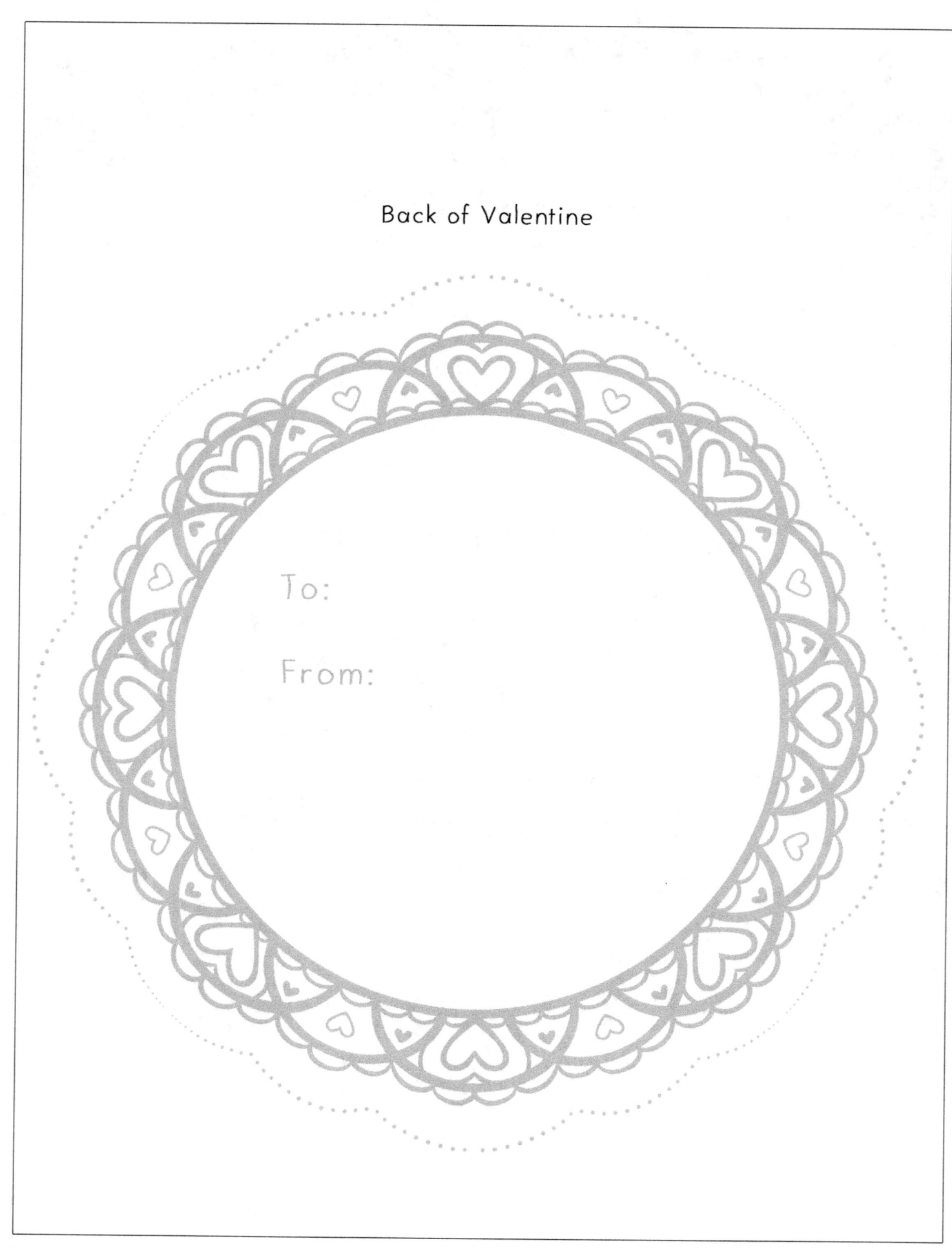

To:

From:

Create a Valentine

Directions: 1. Color Valentine 2. Cut out along dotted line 3. Personlize the back

Happy Valentine's Day!

www.Crafterina.com

Back of Valentine

To:

From:

Create a Heart Valentine

Directions: 1. Color Valentine 2. Cut out along dotted line 3. Personlize the back

Happy Valentine's Day!

Beautiful   dancing.

Bravo!

You're a terrific dance teacher!

Thank you for being a friend!

Back of Valentine

To:

From:

To:

From:

To:

From:

To:

From:

Thank you for being tutu kind!

Ballerina Bestie!

You're my best ballet buddy!

Beautiful dancing!

Happy Valentine's Day!

You're the best ballet teacher!

www.Crafterina.com

Paper Valentine Craft

Directions: 1. Color Valentine 2. Cut out 3. Personlize the back

You're Tutu Sweet!

Happy Valentine's Day!

You're Tutu Cute!

You've Got a Friend in Me!

You are a Dazzling Dancer!

You're Tutu Talented!

Paper Valentine Craft
Back of Cards

Happy Valentine's Day!

To:

From:

Happy Valentine's Day!

To:

From:

Happy Valentine's Day!

To:

From:

Happy Valentine's Day!

To:

From:

Happy Valentine's Day!

To:

From:

Happy Valentine's Day!

To:

From:

Paper Valentine Craft

Directions: 1. Color Valentine 2. Cut out 3. Personlize the back

Lovely Leaping!

Be My Balletine!

Pretty Pirouettes!

Fantastic Flexed Feet!

You're a great dancer!

Terrific Tour en l'air!

Paper Valentine Craft
Back of Cards

Happy Valentine's Day!

To:

From:

Happy Valentine's Day!

To:

From:

Happy Valentine's Day!

To:

From:

Happy Valentine's Day!

To:

From:

Happy Valentine's Day!

To:

From:

Happy Valentine's Day!

To:

From:

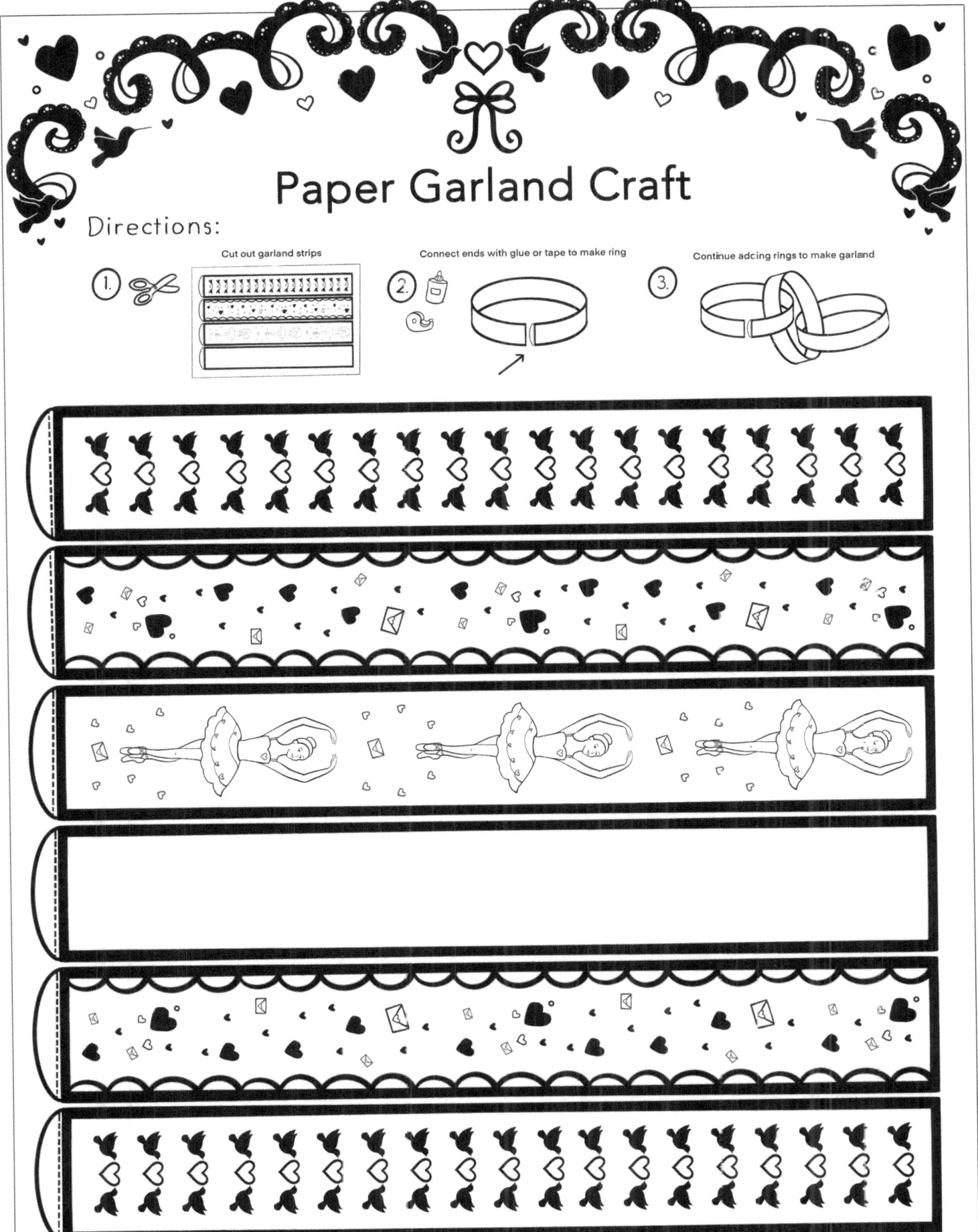

Paper Garland Craft

Directions:

1. Cut out garland strips
2. Connect ends with glue or tape to make ring
3. Continue adcing rings to make garland

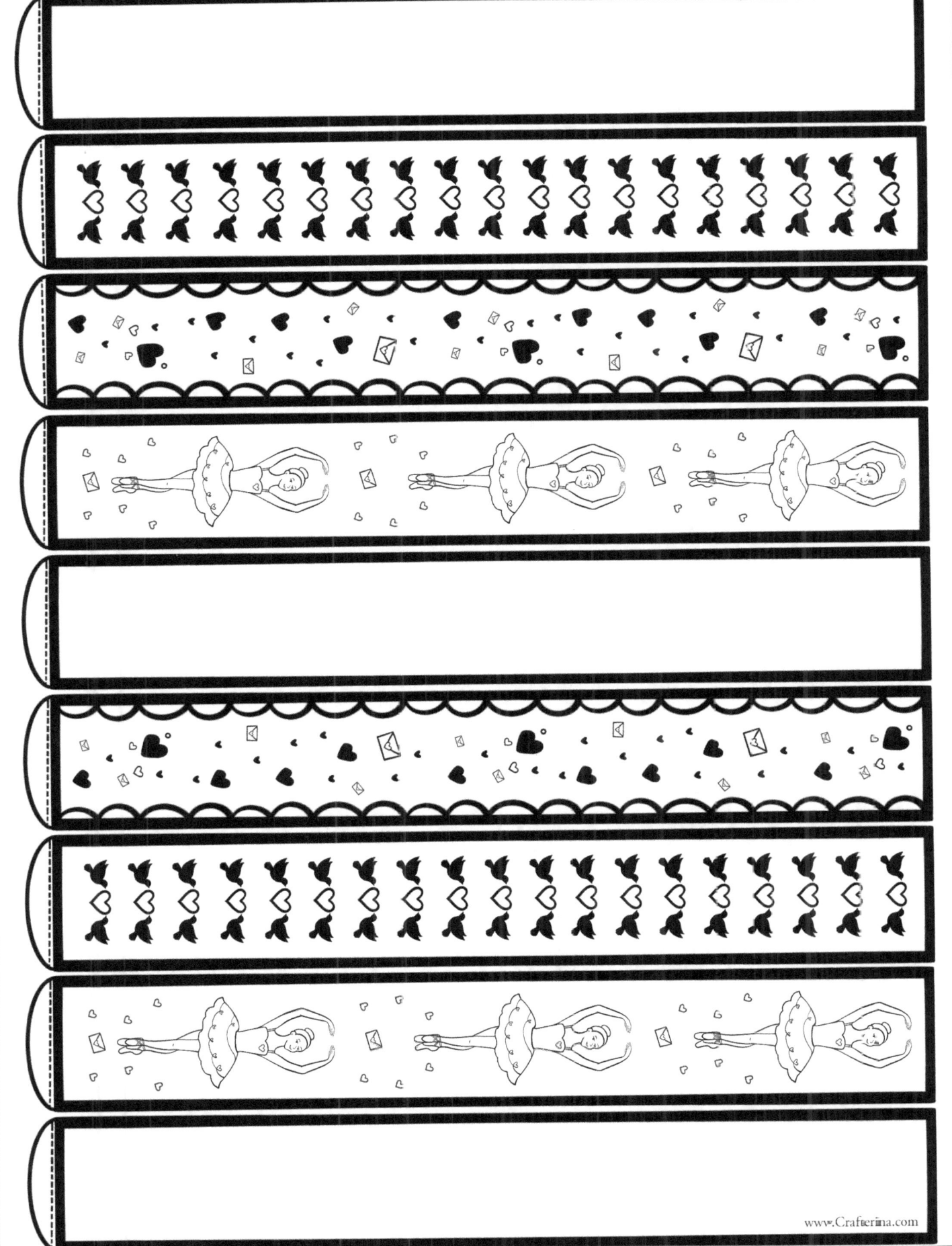

Valentine's Day Pop-Up Card Craft

Happy Valentine's Day!

Front of Card

Back of Card

Inside of Card

Valentine's Day Pop-Up Card Craft

www.Crafterina.com

Valentine's Day Pop-Up Card Craft Directions

Cut out card and tutu template

1.

Outside of card

Accordion fold tutu template along dotted lines
Fold template in half and tape inside center together

2.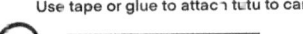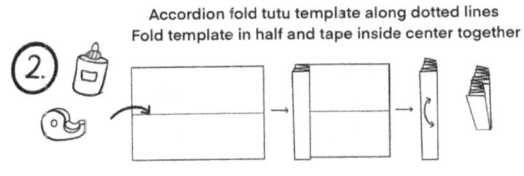

Use tape or glue to attach tutu to card

3.

Inside of card

Tutu Template

www.Crafterina.com

Tiara Paper Craft

Directions:

 — Cut out tiara template
1.

Connect ends with glue or tape to make ring
2.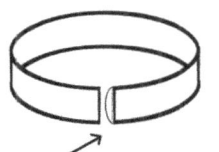

Time to celebrate!
3.

Paper Doll Craft

www.Crafterina.com

Paper Doll Craft

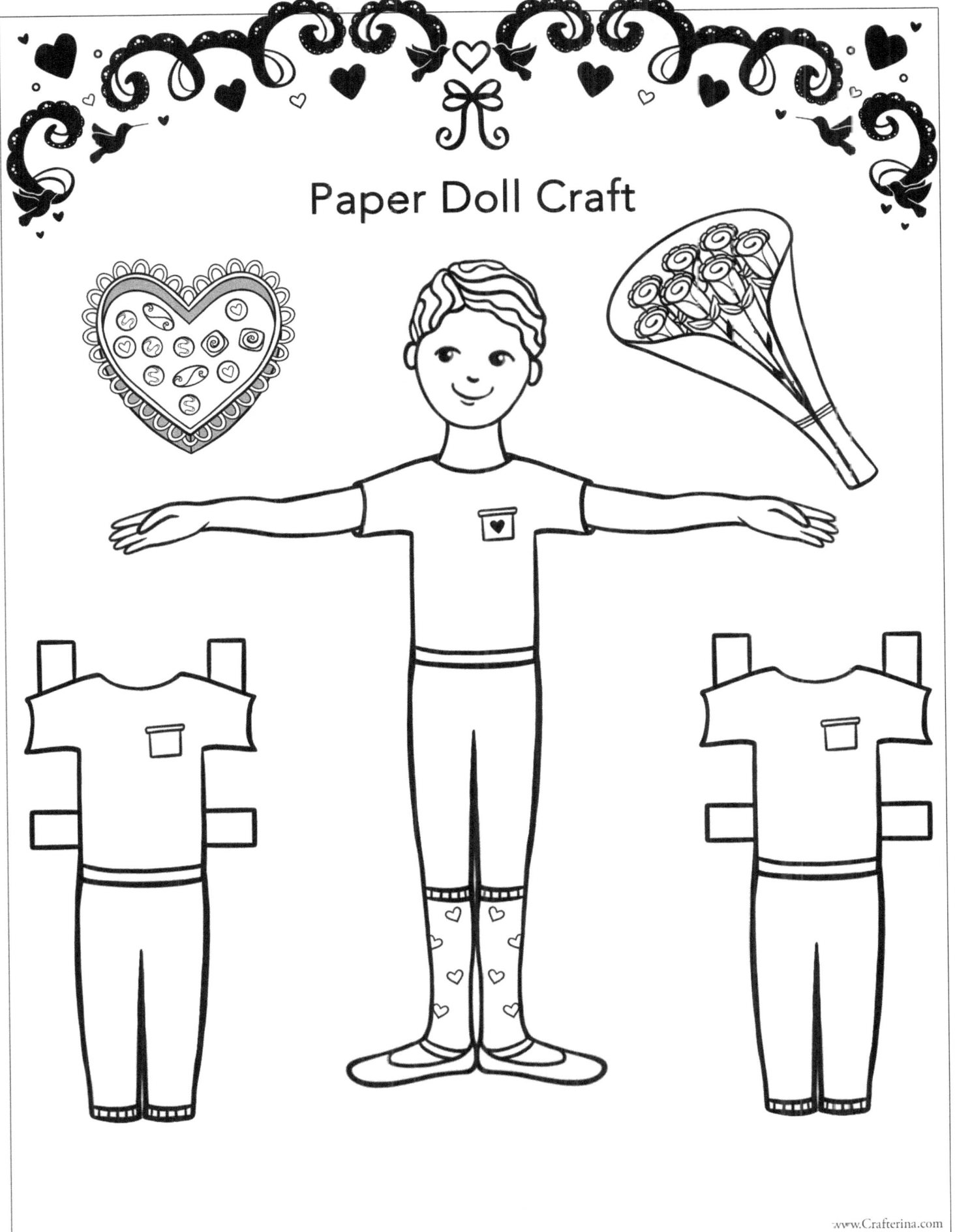

Paper Doll Craft

www.Crafterina.com

About the Author

Vanessa Salgado is a Professional Dancer, Educator and Illustrator.

She has taught many little dancers across Manhattan, concentrating primarily at the Joffrey Ballet School, School at STEPS on Broadway, and Alvin Ailey School. She has also worked as an Associate for the Education Department at New York City Center. Vanessa is a graduate of the Alvin Ailey/Fordham University BFA Program at Lincoln Center and holds a certification in Dance Education. Her work has been featured in Dance Teacher Magazine, Dance Spirit, Dance Informa, and METRO US Newspaper, among others.

Her earliest memories involve story time with her dad, creating with her mom after school, and attending weekend ballet class alongside her sister, Donna. Her interests in visual art revealed themselves wholeheartedly in high school as she simultaneously trained for the professional dance world. As she transitioned into her college days and into her professional life, her incessant doodles and crafting have remained a source of wonder for all those around her.

For more information:
www.VanessaSalgado.com

About Crafterina®

Vanessa is also the creator of Crafterina® a series of dance education books and crafts for families. Designed to spark imagination and inspire movement at home, Crafterina® uniquely incorporates reading, creating and dancing in one. Through this interdisciplinary approach, Crafterina® playfully encourages empowerment and teaches youngsters they have the ability to make anything possible.

Inspire a lifelong love for learning in dance with the help of Crafterina®.

For more information, visit our website for books, crafts, and printables:

www.Crafterina.com

Crafterina

Find more from Crafterina by visiting:
www.Crafterina.com